DOGS SET X

SCOTTISH DEERHOUNDS

Megan M. Gunderson
ABDO Publishing Company

visit us at
www.abdopublishing.com

Published by ABDO Publishing Company, PO Box 398166, Minneapolis, MN 55439.
Copyright © 2013 by Abdo Consulting Group, Inc. International copyrights reserved
in all countries. No part of this book may be reproduced in any form without written
permission from the publisher. The Checkerboard Library™ is a trademark and logo of
ABDO Publishing Company.

Printed in the United States of America, North Mankato, Minnesota.
102012
012013

PRINTED ON RECYCLED PAPER

Cover Photo: Glow Images
Interior Photos: Alamy pp. 10, 13, 15; AP Images p. 19; Corbis pp. 7, 11;
   Glow Images pp. 5, 9; KimballStock p. 20; Klein-Hubert/KimballStock p. 16

Editors: Tamara L. Britton, Stephanie Hedlund
Art Direction: Neil Klinepier

Cataloging-in-Publication Data

Gunderson, Megan M., 1981-
 Scottish deerhounds / Megan M. Gunderson.
   p. cm. -- (Dogs)
Includes bibliographical references and index.
ISBN 978-1-61783-592-6
1. Scottish deerhound--Juvenile literature. 2. Dogs--Juvenile literature. I. Title.
636.7/53--dc23
                                                                    2012946335

CONTENTS

THE DOG FAMILY

In the United States, people care for more than 78 million pet dogs. Some would say their dogs care for them, too! Today, dogs help their owners hunt. They guard people and property. They herd other animals, run races, and guide and calm people.

Dogs and humans have had an important relationship for more than 12,000 years. Scientists believe dogs descended from gray wolves. Like wolves, dogs belong to the family **Canidae**. Over time, humans **domesticated** dogs. And, different **breeds** were developed to help with various tasks.

Some early dogs helped humans rid their grain stores of pests. Others guarded livestock. Scottish deerhounds were bred for hunting. These courageous sight hounds are big enough to hunt deer. Yet they are calm enough to make great pets!

Dog breeds differ in size, shape, and color. It's hard to believe all dogs are the same species, *Canis lupus familiaris!*

SCOTTISH DEERHOUNDS

Scottish deerhounds are one of the oldest dog **breeds**. They have been identified since the 1500s or 1600s. Over time, they have been called Scotch greyhounds, rough greyhounds, and highland deerhounds. They are often confused with Irish wolfhounds.

Scottish deerhounds have long been prized for their amazing hunting abilities. As their name implies, they were deer hunters.

In the early years, no one below the rank of **earl** was allowed to own or breed these dogs. Over time, this led to the breed nearly dying out. Thankfully, breed enthusiasts took over in the early 1800s.

The Scottish deerhound became known as the Royal Dog of Scotland.

Today, deerhounds are still rare. But they are not in danger of disappearing.

The **American Kennel Club (AKC)** recognized the Scottish deerhound in 1886. It is part of the AKC's hound group.

WHAT THEY'RE LIKE

Scottish deerhounds are big and powerful enough to take down deer. Yet they make quiet, devoted pets. They are easy to train and have a good temperament.

This **breed** is generally good with children. Still, their large size may frighten some kids. Scottish deerhounds usually get along with other dogs. However, keep in mind that they may chase small animals.

Scottish deerhounds are sight hounds. As expert hunters, they also excel at coursing events. During these events, they chase a lure through an open field. Lure coursing showcases the **breed**'s speed, **agility**, endurance, and ability to follow a lure. These qualities are prized in a hunting dog.

Lure coursing is a way for a pet deerhound to practice and show off its natural abilities. This event is popular for sight hounds, which chase prey by sight instead relying on scent.

COAT AND COLOR

The Scottish deerhound has a thick, close-lying coat. On the body, neck, and quarters, the coat feels harsh and wiry. But on the belly, head, and chest, it feels quite soft.

A Scottish deerhound looks like it has a slight mustache and beard.

The wiry fur is three to four inches (8 to 10 cm) long. A slight fringe highlights the insides of the legs. There is also longer hair on the bottom side of the tail. The neck features a mane.

Many people picture the Scottish deerhound with a dark blue-gray coat. However, the coat can also be lighter gray, **brindle**, yellow, sandy red, or red **fawn**. And, some coats feature white on the chest, toes, and tip of the tail.

The Scottish deerhound's long, tapered tail nearly reaches the ground.

SIZE

Scottish deerhounds stand out from the crowd because they are large! Male deerhounds measure 30 inches (76 cm) or more from shoulders to toes. They weigh 85 to 110 pounds (39 to 50 kg). Females are at least 28 inches (71 cm) tall. They weigh 75 to 95 pounds (34 to 43 kg).

The Scottish deerhound has a long head. Its **muzzle** tapers to a black or blue nose. The black ears are set high. The dog's keen eyes are brown or hazel.

Broad legs and compact feet support the dog's large body. Its deep chest tells you this **breed** has the lungs of a runner! The long, powerful neck helps the deerhound hunt large prey.

The deerhound's ears have a fold, even if raised in excitement.

CARE

Like any dog, your Scottish deerhound will thrive on love and attention. It won't need a lot of grooming, and it doesn't **shed** very much. Just brush it with a wide-tooth comb when needed. Keep in mind its rough coat is meant to look a little shaggy. And, a deerhound rarely needs a bath.

This **breed** should be exercised once or twice each day. But owners must be careful when outdoors with their deerhounds. Be sure to keep these speedy dogs in fenced areas! And, watch for foot and leg injuries due to running and jumping.

Find a veterinarian familiar with Scottish deerhounds. This is important because the breed can have a hard time with medications. The

veterinarian can also **spay** or **neuter** your pet if puppies are not desired. And, he or she will provide all necessary **vaccines**.

Let your speedy Scottish deerhound run in a safe area. This is a great way for it to get exercise.

FEEDING

Just like you, your dog needs a healthy diet. So choose a complete, balanced dog food for your pet. Some owners also give their deerhounds cooked vegetables or fresh meat.

Keep your dog at a healthy weight. Make sure treats are healthy and given sparingly.

Proper **nutrition** is especially important for puppies. They grow a lot during the first year! Their bones and muscles must develop properly. So, feed them commercial food made especially for puppies.

Scottish deerhounds are big dogs with big appetites. Yet their food should be spread out throughout the day. Adults should be fed two to three times a day. Puppies should have three or more small meals each day.

Be sure your Scottish deerhound always has plenty of fresh water available. Just don't let it gulp water at mealtimes. This will help prevent **bloat**.

The Scottish deerhound's deep chest means bloat is a concern for this **breed**. So, be sure to wait at least an hour after exercise or coursing to feed your dog. And, wait an hour after eating to exercise. Being patient will help avoid this deadly problem.

THINGS THEY NEED

Scottish deerhounds do best when they have a large area for running. Older dogs can do well in apartments. Just make sure your dog gets enough exercise. They make excellent jogging companions!

At home, provide a crate for your dog. It's a cozy place to play quietly with a toy or sleep. It can also help with housebreaking. Pad it with soft bedding so your dog is comfortable.

Toys are a must, too. Be sure they are too large to be swallowed. Safe chew toys will make your possessions less tempting, especially for puppies.

Another key to keeping your dog safe is having it wear a collar with tags. License and identification tags make it easier to return your dog if it is lost. **Microchips** placed under the skin are another option.

A Scottish deerhound named Hickory won Best in Show at the Westminster Kennel Club Dog Show in 2011.

PUPPIES

Have you decided a Scottish deerhound is the perfect dog for your family? If you have the space and time to care for this special **breed**, then it's time to find a reputable breeder. This will ensure you come home with a healthy, happy puppy.

Good breeders care where their pets

Mother dogs are pregnant for about 63 days. Usually, Scottish deerhounds give birth to eight puppies per litter.

find homes. Be prepared to answer lots of questions about where your dog will be living! You should ask lots of questions, too. Good **breeders** can tell you what **vaccines** puppies have received. And, he or she will know of any other health concerns.

The puppy you choose to make part of your family should have bright, clear eyes. Its fur should be clean, and it should be alert and friendly. Usually, breeders will allow you to visit your puppy between five and six weeks of age. By eight to ten weeks of age, a puppy is ready to go home with you.

Scottish deerhound puppies are energetic and curious. Train your puppy early and you will have a quiet, well-mannered pet that loves to be around you. **Socialize** it and you will give it the best chance at a happy life. Your Scottish deerhound will be a devoted companion for 8 to 11 years.

GLOSSARY

agility - the ability to move quickly and easily.

American Kennel Club (AKC) - an organization that studies and promotes interest in purebred dogs.

bloat - a condition in which food and gas trapped in a dog's stomach cause pain, shock, and even death.

breed - a group of animals sharing the same ancestors and appearance. A breeder is a person who raises animals. Raising animals is often called breeding them.

brindle - having dark streaks or spots on a gray, tan, or tawny background.

Canidae (KAN-uh-dee) - the scientific Latin name for the dog family. Members of this family are called canids. They include wolves, jackals, foxes, coyotes, and domestic dogs.

domesticated - adapted to life with humans.

earl - a British noble. An earl ranks above a viscount and below a marquess.

fawn - a light grayish brown color.

microchip - an electronic circuit placed under an animal's skin. A microchip contains identifying information that can be read by a scanner.

muzzle - an animal's nose and jaws.

neuter (NOO-tuhr) - to remove a male animal's reproductive glands.

nutrition - that which promotes growth, provides energy, repairs body tissues, and maintains life.

shed - to cast off hair, feathers, skin, or other coverings or parts by a natural process.

socialize - to adapt an animal to behaving properly around people or other animals in various settings.

spay - to remove a female animal's reproductive organs.

vaccine (vak-SEEN) - a shot given to prevent illness or disease.

WEB SITES

To learn more about Scottish deerhounds, visit ABDO Publishing Company online. Web sites about Scottish deerhounds are featured on our Book Links page. These links are routinely monitored and updated to provide the most current information available.

www.abdopublishing.com

23

INDEX